Oscar Wilde

The Soul of Man Under Socialism

Charles H. Kerr Publishing Company
Chicago
1984

Oscar Wilde Around 1900: Drawing by Arthur Cravan

THE SOUL OF MAN
UNDER SOCIALISM

THE chief advantage that would result from the establishment of Socialism is, undoubtedly, the fact that Socialism would relieve us from that sordid necessity of living for others which, in the present condition of things, presses so hardly upon almost everybody. In fact, scarcely anyone at all escapes.

Now and then, in the course of the century, a great man of science, like Darwin; a great poet, like Keats; a fine critical spirit, like M. Renan; a supreme artist, like Flaubert, has been able to isolate himself, to keep himself out of reach of the clamorous claims of others, to stand "under the shelter of the wall," as Plato puts it, and so to realize the perfection of what was in him, to his own incomparable gain, and to the incomparable and lasting gain of the whole world. These, however, are exceptions. The majority of people spoil their lives by an unhealthy and exaggerated altruism—are forced, indeed, so to spoil them. They find themselves surrounded by hideous poverty, by hideous ugliness, by hideous starvation. It is inevitable that they should be strongly moved by all this. The emotions of man are stirred more quickly than man's intelligence; and, as I pointed out some time ago in an article on the function of criticism, it is much more easy to have sympathy with suffering than it is to have sympathy with thought. Accordingly, with admirable, though misdirected intentions, they very seriously and very sentimentally set themselves to the task of remedying the evils that they see. But their remedies do not cure the disease: they merely prolong it. Indeed, their remedies are part of the disease.

They try to solve the problem of poverty, for instance, by keeping the poor alive; or, in the case of a very advanced school, by amusing the poor.

But this is not a solution: it is an aggravation of the difficulty. The proper aim is to try and reconstruct society on such a basis that poverty will be impossible. And the altruistic virtues have really prevented the carrying out of this aim. Just as the worst slave-owners were those who were kind to their slaves, and so prevented the horror of the system being realized by those who suffered from it, and understood by those who contemplated it, so, in the present state of things in England, the people who do most harm are the people who try to do most good; and at last we have had the spectacle of men who have really

studied the problem and know the life—
educated men who live in the East End
—coming forward and imploring the community to restrain its altruistic impulses of
charity, benevolence, and the like. They
do so on the ground that such charity degrades and demoralizes. They are perfectly
right. Charity creates a multitude of sins.

There is also this to be said. It is immoral to use private property in order to
alleviate the horrible evils that result from
the institution of private property. It is
both immoral and unfair.

Under Socialism all this will, of course,
be altered. There will be no people living
in fetid dens and fetid rags, and bringing
up unhealthy, hunger-pinched children in
the midst of impossible and absolutely repulsive surroundings. The security of society will not depend, as it does now, on
the state of the weather. If a frost comes
we shall not have a hundred thousand men
out of work, tramping about the streets in
a state of disgusting misery, or whining to
their neighbors for alms, or crowding round
the doors of loathsome shelters to try and
secure a hunch of bread and a night's unclean lodging. Each member of the society
will share in the general prosperity and
happiness of the society, and if a frost
comes no one will practically be anything
the worse.

Upon the other hand, Socialism itself will

be of value simply because it will lead to individualism.

Socialism, Communism, or whatever one chooses to call it, by converting private property into public wealth, and substituting co-operation for competition, will restore society to its proper condition of a thoroughly healthy organism, and insure the material well-being of each member of the community. It will, in fact, give Life its proper basis and its proper environment. But for the full development of Life to its highest mode of perfection, something more is needed. What is needed is Individualism. If the Socialism is Authoritarian; if there are Governments armed with economic power as they are now with political power; if, in a word, we are to have Industrial Tyrannies, then the last state of man will be worse than the first. At present, in consequence of the existence of private property, a great many people are enabled to develop a certain very limited amount of Individualism. They are either under no necessity to work for their living, or are enabled to choose the sphere of activity that is really congenial to them, and gives them pleasure. These are the poets, the philosophers, the men of science, the men of culture—in a word, the real men, the men who have realized themselves, and in whom all Humanity gains a partial realization. Upon the other hand, there are a great many people who, having no private property of their own, and being always on the brink of sheer starvation, are compelled to do the work of beasts of burden, to do work that is quite uncongenial to them, and to which they are forced by the peremptory, unreasonable, degrading Tyranny of want. These are the poor, and amongst them there is no grace of manner, or charm of speech, or civilization, or culture, or refinement in pleasures, or joy of life. From their collective force Humanity gains much in material prosperity. But it is only the material result that it gains, and the man who is poor is in himself absolutely of no importance. He is merely the infinitesmal atom of a force that, so far from regarding him, crushes him: indeed, prefers him crushed, as in that case he is far more obedient.

Of course, it might be said that the Individualism generated under conditions of private property is not always, or even as a rule, of a fine or wonderful type, and that the poor, if they have not culture and charm, have still many virtues. Both these statements would be quite true. The possession of private property is very often extremely demoralizing, and that is, of course, one of the reasons why Socialism wants to get rid of the institution. In fact, property is really a nuisance. Some years ago people went about the country saying that property has duties. They said

it so often and so tediously that, at last,
the Church has begun to say it. One hears
it now from every pulpit. It is perfectly
true. Property not merely has duties, but
has so many duties that its possession to
any large extent is a bore. It involves
endless claims upon one, endless attention
to business, endless bother. If property
had simply pleasures, we could stand it.;
but its duties make it unbearable. In the
interest of the rich we must get rid of it.
The virtues of the poor may be readily admitted, and are much to be regretted. We
are often told that the poor are grateful
for charity. Some of them are, no doubt,
but the best amongst the poor are never
grateful. They are ungrateful, discontented, disobedient, and rebellious. They are
quite right to be so. Charity they feel to
be a ridiculously inadequate mode of partial restitution, or a sentimental dole, usu-
ally accompanied by some impertinent attempt on the part of the sentimentalist to
tyrannize over their private lives. Why
should they be grateful for the crumbs that
fall from the rich man's table? They should
be seated at the board, and are beginning
to know it. As for being discontented, a
man who would not be discontented with
such surroundings and such a low mode of
life would be a perfect brute. Disobedience, in the eyes of anyone who has read
history, is man's original virtue. It is

through disobedience that progress has been made, through disobedience and through rebellion. Sometimes the poor are praised for being thrifty. But to recommend thrift to the poor is both grotesque and insulting. It is like advising a man who is starving to eat less. For a town or country laborer to practice thrift, would be absolutely immoral. Man should not be ready to show that he can live like a badly-fed animal. He should decline to live like that, and should either steal or go on the rates, which is considered by many to be a form of stealing. As for begging, it is safer to beg than to take, but it is finer to take than to beg. No: a poor man who is ungrateful, unthrifty, discontented, and rebellious, is probably a real personality, and has much in him. He is at any rate a healthy protest. As for the virtuous poor, one can pity them, of course, but one cannot possibly admire them. They have made private terms with the enemy, and sold their birthright for very bad pottage. They must also be extraordinarily stupid. I can quite understand a man accepting laws that protect private property, and admit of its accumulation, as long as he himself is able under those conditions to realize some form of beautiful and intellectual life. But it is almost incredible to me how a man whose life is marred and made hideous by such laws can possibly acquiesce in their continuance.

However, the explanation is not really difficult to find. It is simply this. Misery and poverty are so absolutely degrading, and exercise such a paralyzing effect over the nature of men, that no class is ever really conscious of its own suffering. They have to be told of it by other people, and they often entirely disbelieve them. What is said by great employers of labor against agitators is unquestionably true. Agitators are a set of interfering, meddling people, who come down to some perfectly contented class of the community, and sow the seeds of discontent amongst them. That is the reason why agitators are so absolutely necessary. Without them, in our incomplete state, there would be no advance towards civilization. Slavery was put down in America, not in consequence of any action on the part of the slaves, or even any express desire on their part that they should be free. It was put down entirely through the grossly illegal conduct of certain agitators in Boston and elsewhere, who were not slaves themselves, nor owners of slaves, nor had anything to do with the question really. It was, undoubtedly, the Abolitionists who set the torch alight, who began the whole thing. And it is curious to note that from the slaves themselves they received, not merely very little assistance, but hardly any sympathy even; and when at the close of the war the slaves found themselves free, found themselves inded so absolutely free that they were free to starve, many of them bitterly regretted the new state of things. To the thinker, the most tragic fact in the whole of the French Revolution is not that Marie Antoinette was killed for being a queen, but that the starved peasant of the Vendee voluntarily went out to die for the hideous cause of feudalism.

It is clear, then, that no Authoritarian Socialism will do. For while under the present system a very large number of people can lead lives of a certain amount of freedom and expression and happiness, under an industrial-barrack system, or a system of economic tyranny, nobody would be able to have any such freedom at all. It is to be regretted that a portion of our community should be practically in slavery, but to propose to solve the problem by enslaving the entire community is childish. Every man must be left quite free to choose his own work. No form of compulsion must be exercised over him. If there is, his work will not be good for him, will not be good in itself, and will not be good for others. And by work I simply mean activity of any kind.

I hardly think that any Socialist, nowadays, would seriously propose that an inspector should call every morning at each house to see that each citizen rose up and did manual labor for eight hours. Humanity has got beyond that stage, and reserves such a form of life for the people whom, in a very arbitrary manner, it chooses to call criminals. But I confess that many of the socialistic views that I have come across seem to me to be tainted with ideas of authority, if not of actual compulsion. Of course, authority and compulsion are out of the question. All association must be quite voluntary. It is only in voluntary associations that man is fine.

But it may be asked how Individualism, which is now more or less dependent on the existence of private property for its development, will benefit by the abolition of such private property. The answer is very simple. It is true, that under existing conditions, a few men who have had private means of their own, such as Byron, Shelley, Browning, Victor Hugo, Baudelaire, and others, have been able to realize their personality more or less completely. Not one of these men ever did a single day's work for hire. They were relieved from poverty. They had an immense advantage. The question is whether it would be for the good of Individualism that such an advantage should be taken away. Let us suppose that it is taken away.

What happens then to Individualism? How will it benefit?

It will benefit in this way. Under the new conditions Individualism will be far freer, far finer, and far more intensified than it is now. I am not talking of the great imaginatively-realized Individualism of such poets as I have mentioned, but of the great actual Individualism latent and potential in mankind generally. For the recognition of private property has really harmed Individualism, and obscured it, by confusing a man with what he possesses. It has led Individualism entirely astray. It has made gain not growth its aim. So that man thought that the important thing was to have, and did not know that the important thing is to be. The true prefection of man lies, not in what man has, but in what man is. Private property has crushed true Individualism, and set up an Individualism that is false. It has debarred one part of the community from being individual by starving them. It has debarred the other part of the community from being individual by putting them on the wrong road, and encumbering them. Indeed, so completely has man's personality been absorbed by his possessions that the English law has always treated offences against a man's property with far more severity than offences against his person, and property is still the test of complete citizenship. The industry necessary for the making money is also very demoralizing. In a community like ours, where property confers immense distinction, social position, honor, respect, titles, and other pleasant things of the kind, man, being naturally ambitious, makes it his aim to accumulate this property, and goes on wearily and tediously accumulating it long after he has got far more than he wants, or can use, or enjoy, or perhaps even know of. Man will kill himself by overwork in order to secure property, and really, considering the enormous advantages that property brings, one is hardly surprised. One's regret is that society should be constructed on such a basis that man has been forced into a groove in which he cannot freely develop what is wonderful, and fascinating, and delightful in him—in which, in fact, he misses the true pleasure and joy of living. He is also, under existing conditions, very insecure. An enormously wealthy merchant may be—often is—at every moment of his life at the mercy of things that are not under his control. If the wind blows an extra point or so, or the weather suddenly changes, or some trivial thing happens, his ship may go down, his speculations may go wrong, and he finds himself a poor man, with his social position quite gone. Now, nothing should be able to harm a man except himself. Nothing should be able to rob a man at all. What a man really has, is what is in him. What is outside of him should be a matter of no importance.

With the abolition of private property, then, we shall have true, beautiful healthy Individualism. Nobody will waste his life in accumulating things, and the symbols for things. One will live. To live is the rarest thing in the world. Most people exist, that is all.

It is a question whether we have ever seen the full expression of a personality, except on the imaginative plane of art. In action, we never have. Cæsar, says Mommsen, was the complete and perfect man. But how tragically insecure was Cæsar! Wherever there is a man who exercises authority, there is a man who resists authority. Cæsar was very perfect, but his perfection traveled by too dangerous a road. Marcus Aurelius was the perfect man, says Renan. Yes; the great emperor was a perfect man. But how intolerable were the endless claims upon him! He staggered under the burden of the empire. He was conscious how inadequate one man was to bear the weight of that Titan and too vast orb. What I mean by a perfect man is one who develops under perfect conditions; one who is not wounded, or worried, or maimed, or in danger. Most personalities have been obliged to be rebels. Half their strength has been wasted in friction. Byron's personality for instance, was terribly wasted in its battle with the stupidity, and hypocrisy, and Philistinism of the English. Such battles do not always intensify strength: they often exaggerate weakness. Byron was never able to give us what he might have given us. Shelley escaped better. Like Byron, he got out of England as soon as possible. But he was not so well known. If the English had had any idea of what a great poet he really was, they would have fallen on him with tooth and nail, and made his life as unbearable to him as they possibly could. But he was not a remarkable figure in society and consequently he escaped, to a certain degree. Still, even in Shelley the note of rebellion is sometimes too strong. The note of the perfect personality is not rebellion, but peace.

It will be a marvelous thing—the true personality of man—when we see it. It will grow naturally and simply, flowerlike, or as a tree grows. It will not be at discord. It will never argue or dispute. It will not prove things. It will know everything. And yet it will not busy itself about knowledge. It will have wisdom. Its value will not be measured by material things. It will have nothing. And yet it will have everything, and whatever one takes from it, it will still have, so rich will it be. It will not be always meddling with others, or asking them to be like itself. It will love them because they will be different. And yet while it will not meddle with others it will help all, as a beautiful thing helps us, by being what it is. The personality of man will be very wonderful. It will be as wonderful as the personality of a child.

In its development it will be assisted by Christianity, if men desire that; but if men do not desire that, it will develop none the less surely. For it will not worry itself about the past, nor care whether things happened or did not happen. Nor will it admit any laws but its own laws; nor any authority but its own authority. Yet it will love those who sought to intensify it, and speak often of them. And of these Christ was one.

"Know thyself" was written over the portal of the antique world. Over the portal of the new world, "Be thyself" shall be written. And the messages of Christ to man was simply "Be thyself." That is the secret of Christ.

When Jesus talks about the poor he simply means personalities, just as when he talks about the rich he simply means people who have not developed their personalities. Jesus moved in a community that allowed the accumulation of private property just as ours does, and the gospel that he preached was not that in such a community it is an advantage for a man to live on scanty, unwholesome food, to wear ragged, unwholesome clothes, to sleep in horrid, unwholesome dwellings, and a disadvantage for a man to live under healthy, pleasant, and decent conditions. Such a view would have been wrong there and then, and would, of course, be still more wrong now and in England; for as man moves northward the material necessities of life become of more vital importance, and our society is infinitely more complex, and displays far greater extremes of luxury and pauperism than any society of the antique world. What Jesus meant was this. He said to man, "You have a wonderful personality. Develop it. Be yourself. Don't imagine that your perfection lies in accumulating or possessing external things. Your perfection is inside of you. If only you could realize that, you would not want to be rich. Ordinary riches can be stolen from a man. Real riches cannot. In the treasury-house of your soul, there are infinitely precious things, that may not be taken from you. And so, try to so shape your life that external things will not harm you. And try also to get rid of personal property. It involves sordid preoccupation, endless industry, continual wrong. Personal property hinders Individualism at every step." It is to be noted that Jesus never says that impoverished people are necessarily good, or wealthy people necessarily bad. That would not have been true. Wealthy people are, as a class, better than impoverished people, more moral, more intellectual, more well-behaved. There is only one class in the community that thinks more about money than the rich, and that is the poor. The poor can think of nothing else. That is the misery of being poor. What Jesus does say is that man reaches his perfection, not through what he has, not even through what he does, but entirely through what he is. And so the wealthy young man who comes to Jesus is represented as a thoroughly good citizen, who has broken none of the laws of his state, none of the commandments of his religion. He is quite respectable, in the ordinary sense of that extraordinary word. Jesus says to him, "You should give up private property. It hinders you from realizing your perfection. It is a drag upon you. It is a burden. Your personality does not need it. It is within you, and not outside of you, that you will find what you really are, and what you really want." To his own friends he says the same thing. He tells them to be themselves, and not to be always worrying about other things. What do other things matter? Man is complete in himself. When they go into the world, the world will disagree with them. That is inevitable. The world hates Individualism. But that is not to trouble them. They are to be calm and self-centred. If a man takes their cloak, they are to give him their coat, just to show that material things are of no importance. If people abuse them, they are not to answer back. What does it signify? The things people say of a man do not alter a man. He is what he is. Public opinion is of no value whatsoever. Even if people employ actual violence, they are not to be violent in turn. That would be to fall to the same low level. After all, even in prison, a man can be quite free. His soul can be free. His personalities can be untroubled. He can be at peace. And, above all things, they are not to interfere with other people or judge them in any way. Personality is a very mysterious thing. A man cannot always be estimated by what he does. He may keep the law, and yet be worthless. He may break the law, and yet be fine. He may be bad, without ever doing anything bad. He may commit a sin against society, and yet realize through that sin his true perfection.

There was a woman who was taken in adultery. We are not told the history of her love, but that love must have been very great; for Jesus said that her sins were forgiven her, not because she repented, but because her love was so intense and wonderful. Later on, a short time before his death, as he sat at a feast, the woman came

in and poured costly perfumes on his hair.
His friends tried to interfere with her, and
said that it was an extravagance, and that
the money that the perfume cost should
have been expended on charitable relief of
people in want, or something of that kind.
Jesus did not accept that view. He pointed
out that the material needs of Man were
great and very permanent, but that the
spiritual needs of Man were greater still,
and that in one divine moment, and be se-
lecting its own mode of expression, a personality might make itself perfect. The
world worships the woman, even now, as
a saint.

Yes; there are suggestive things in Individualism. Socialism annihilates family
life, for instance. With the abolition of private property, marriage in its present form
must disappear. This is part of the pro-
gram. Individualism accepts this and
makes it fine. It converts the abolition of
legal restraint into a form of freedom that
will help the full development of personality, and make the love of man and woman
more wonderful, more beautiful, and more
ennobling. Jesus knew this. He rejected
the claims of family life, although they
existed in his day and community in a very
marked form. "Who is my mother. Who
are my brothers?" he said, when he was
told that they wished to speak to him.
When one of his followers asked leave to

go and bury his father, "Let the dead bury the dead," was his terrible answer. He would allow no claim whatsoever to be made on personality.

And so he who would lead a Christ-like life is he who is perfectly and absolutely himself. He may be a great poet, or a great man of science; or a young student at a University, or one who watches sheep upon a moor; or a maker of dramas, like Shakespeare, or a thinker about God, like Spinoza; or a child who plays in a garden, or a fisherman who throws his net into the sea. It does not matter what he is, as long as he realizes the perfection of the soul that is within him. All imitation in morals and in life is wrong. Through the streets of Jerusalem at the present day crawls one who is mad and carries a wooden cross on his shoulders. He is a symbol of the lives that are marred by imitation. Father Damien was Christlike when he went out to live with the lepers, because in such service he realized fully what was best in him. But he was not more Christlike than Wagner when he realized his soul in music; or than Shelley, when he realized his soul in song. There is no one type for man. There are as many perfections as there are imperfect men. And while to the claims of charity a man may yield and yet be free, to the claims of conformity no man may yield and remain free at all.

Individualism, then, is what through Socialism we are to attain to. As a natural result the State must give up all idea of government. It must give it up because, as a wise man once said many centuries before Christ, there is such a thing as leaving mankind alone; there is no such thing as governing mankind. All modes of government are failures. Despotism is unjust to everybody, including the despot, who was probably made for better things. Oligarchies are unjust to the many, and ochlocracies are unjust to the few. High hopes were once formed of democracy; but democracy means simply the bludgeoning of the people by the people for the people. It has been found out. I must say that it was high time, for all authority is quite degrading. It degrades those who exercise it, and degrades those over whom it is exercised. When it is violently, grossly, and cruelly used, it produces a good effect, by creating, or at any rate bringing out, the spirit of revolt and Individualism that is to kill it. When it is used with a certain amount of kindness, and accompanied by prizes and rewards, it is dreadfully demoralizing. People, in that case, are less conscious of the horrible pressure that is being put on them, and so go through their lives in a sort of coarse comfort, like petted animals, without ever realizing that they are probably thinking other people's thoughts, living by other people's standards, wearing practically what one may call other people's second-hand clothes, and never being themselves for a single moment. "He who would be free," says a fine thinker, "must not conform." And authority, by bribing people to conform, produces a very gross kind of over-fed barbarism amongst us.

With authority, punishment will pass away. This will be a great gain—a gain, in fact, of incalculable value. As one reads history, not in the expurgated editions written for schoolboys and passmen, but in the original authorities of each time, one is absolutely sickened, not by the crimes that the wicked have committed, but by the punishments that the good have inflicted; and a community is infinitely more brutalized by the habitual employment of punishment, than it is by the occurrence of crime. It obviously follows that the more punishment is inflicted the more crime is produced, and most modern legislation has clearly recognized this, and has made it its task to diminish punishment as far as it thinks it can. Wherever it has really diminished it, the results have always been extremely good. The less punishment, the less crime. When there is no punishment at all, crime will either cease to exist, or, if it occurs, will be treated by physicians as a very distressing form of dementia, to be cured by care and kindness. For what are called criminals nowadays are not criminals at all. Starvation, and not sin, is the parent of modern crime. That indeed is the reason why our criminals are, as a class, so absolutely uninteresting from any psychological point of view. They are not marvellous Macbeths and terrible Vautrins. They are merely what ordinary, respectable, commonplace people would be if they had not got enough to eat. When private property is abolished there will be no necessity for crime, no demand for it; it will cease to exist. Of course, all crimes are not crimes against property, though such are the crimes that the English law, valuing what a man has more than what a man is, punishes with the harshest and most horrible severity, if we except the crime of murder, and regard death as worse than penal servitude, a point on which our criminals, I believe, disagree. But though a crime may not be against property, it may spring from the misery and rage and depression produced by our wrong system of property-holding, and so, when that system is abolished, will disappear. When each member of the community has sufficient for his wants, and is not interfered with by his neighbor, it will not be an object of any interest to him to interfere with anyone else. Jealousy, which is an extraordinary source of crime in modern life, is an emotion closely bound up with our conceptions of property, and under Socialism and Individualism will die out. It is remarkable that in communistic tribes jealousy is entirely unknown.

Now as the State is not to govern, it may be asked what the State is to do. The State is to be a voluntary association that will organize labor, and be the manufacturer and distributer of necessary commodities. The State is to make what is useful. The individual is to make what is beautiful. And as I have mentioned the word labor, I cannot help saying that a great deal of nonsense is being written and talked nowadays about the dignity of manual labor. There is nothing necessarily dignified about manual labor at all, and most of it is absolutely degrading. It is mentally and morally injurious to man to do anything in which he does not find pleasure, and many forms of labor are quite pleasureless activities, and should be regarded as such. To sweep a slushy crossing for eight hours on a day when the east wind is blowing is a disgusting occupation. To sweep it with mental, moral, or physical dignity seems to me to be impossible. To sweep it with joy would be appalling. Man is made for something better than disturbing dirt. All work of that kind should be done by a machine.

And I have no doubt that it will be so.

Up to the present, man has been, to a certain extent, the slave of machinery, and there is something tragic in the fact that as soon as man had invented a machine to do his work he began to starve. This, however, is, of course, the result of our property system and our system of competition. One man owns a machine which does the work of five hundred men. Five hundred men are, in consequence, thrown out of employment, and, having no work to do, become hungry and take to thieving. The one man secures the produce of the machine and keeps it, and has five hundred times as much as he should have, and probably, which is of much more importance, a great deal more than he really wants. Were that machine the property of all, everyone would benefit by it. It would be an immense advantage to the community. All unintellectual labor, all monotonous, dull labor, all labor that deals with dreadful things, and involves unpleasant conditions, must be done by machinery. Machinery must work for us in coal mines, and do all sanitary services, and be the stoker of steamers, and clean streets, and run messages on wet days, and do anything that is tedious or distressing. At present machinery competes against man. Under proper conditions machinery will serve man. There is no doubt at all that this is the future of machinery, and just as trees grow while the country gentleman is asleep, so while Humanity will be amusing itself, or enjoying cultivated leisure—which, and not labor, is the aim of man—or making beautiful things, or reading beautiful things, or simply contemplating the world with admiration and delight, machinery will be doing all the necessary and unpleasant work. The fact is, that civilization requires slaves. The Greeks were quite right there. Unless there are slaves to do the ugly, horrible, uninteresting work, culture and contemplation become almost impossible. Human slavery is wrong, insecure, and demoralizing. On mechanical slavery, on the slavery of the machine, the future of the world depends. And when scientific men are no longer called upon to go down to a depressing East End and distribute bad cocoa and worse blankets to starving people, they will have delightful leisure in which to devise wonderful and marvelous things for their own joy and the joy of everyone else. There will be great storages of force for every city, and for every house if required, and this force man will convert into heat, light, or motion, according to his needs. Is this Utopian? A map of the world that does not include Utopia is not worth even glancing at, for it leaves out the one country at which Humanity is always landing. And when Humanity lands there, it looks out, and, seeing a better country, sets sail. Progress is the realization of Utopias.

Now, I have said that the community by means of organization of machinery will supply the useful things and that the beautiful things will be made by the individual. This is not merely necessary, but it is the only possible way by which we can get either the one or the other. An individual who has to make things for the use of others, and with reference to their wants and their wishes, does not work with interest, and consequently cannot put into his work what is best in him. Upon the other hand, whenever a community or a powerful section of a community, or a government of any kind, attempts to dictate to the artist what he is to do, Art either entirely vanishes, or becomes stereotyped, or degenerates into a low and ignoble form of craft. A work of art is the unique result of a unique temperament. Its beauty comes from the fact that the author is what he is. It has nothing to do with the fact that other people want what they want. Indeed, the moment that an artist takes notice of what other people want, and tries to supply the demand, he ceases to be an artist, and becomes a dull or an amusing craftsman, an honest or a dishonest tradesman. He has no further claim to be considered as an artist. Art is the most intense mode of Individualism that the world has known. I am inclined to say that it is the only real mode of Individualism that the world has known. Crime, which, under certain conditions, may seem to have created Individualism, must take cognizance of other people and interfere with them. It belongs to the sphere of action. But alone, without any reference to his neighbors, without any interference, the artist can fashion a beautiful thing; and if he does not do it solely for his own pleasure, he is not an artist at all.

And it is to be noted that it is the fact that Art is this intense form of Individualism that makes the public try to exercise over it an authority that is as immoral as it is contemptible. It is not quite their fault. The public has always, and in every age, been badly brought up. They are continually asking art to be popular, to please their want of taste, to flatter their absurd vanity, to tell them what they have been told before, to show them what they ought to be tired of seeing, to amuse them when they feel heavy after eating too much, and to distract their thoughts when they are wearied of their own stupidity. Now Art should never try to be popular. The public should try to make itself artistic. There is a very wide difference. If a man of science were told that the results of his experiments, and the conclusions that he arrived at, should be of such character that they would not upset the received popular notions on the subject, or disturb popular prejudice, or hurt the sensibilities of people who knew nothing about science; if a philosopher were told that he had a perfect right to speculate in the highest spheres of thought, provided that he arrived at the same conclusions as were held by those who had never thought in any sphere at all— well, nowadays the man of science and the philosopher would be considerably amused. Yet, it is really a very few years since both philosophy and science were subjected to brutal popular control, to authority in fact —the authority of either the general ignorance of the community, or the terror and greed for power of an ecclesiastical or governmental class. Of course, we have to a very great extent got rid of any attempt on the part of the community, or the Church, or the Government, to interfere with the individualism of speculative thought, but the attempt to interfere with the individualism of imaginative art still lingers. In fact, it does more than linger; it is aggressive, offensive, and brutalizing.

In England, the arts that have escaped best are the arts in which the public take no interest. Poetry is an instance of what I mean. We have been able to have fine poetry in England because the public do not read it, and consequently do not influence it. The public like to insult poets because they are individual, but once they have insulted them, they leave them alone. In the case of the novel and the drama, arts in which the public do take an interest, the result of the exercise of popular authority has been absolutely ridiculous. No country produces such badly-written fiction, such tedious, common work in the novel form, such silly, vulgar plays as England. It must necessarily be so. The popular standard is of such character that no artist can get to it. It is at once too easy and too difficult to be a popular novelist. It is too easy, because the requirements of the public as far as plot, style, psychology, treatment of life, and treatment of literature are concerned are within the reach of the very meanest capacity and the most uncultivated mind. It is too difficult, because to meet such requirements the artist would have to do violence to his temperament, would have to write not for the artistic joy of writing, but for the amusement of half-educated people, and so would have to suppress his individualism, forget his culture, annihilate his style, and surrender everything that is valuable in him. In the case of the drama, things are a little better; the theater-going public like the obvious, it is true, but they do not like the tedious; and burlesque and farcial comedy, the two most popular forms, are distinct forms of art. Delightful work may be produced under burlesque and farcial conditions, and in work of this kind the artist in England is allowed very great freedom. It is when one comes to the higher forms of the drama that the result of popular control is seen. The one thing that the public dislike is novelty. Any attempt to extend the subject-matter of art is extremely distasteful to the public; and yet the vitality and progress of art depend in a large measure on the continual extension of subject-matter. The public dislike novelty because they are afraid of it. It represents to them a mode of Individualism, an assertion on the part of the artist that he selects his own subject, and treats it as he chooses. The public are quite right in their attitude. Art is Individualism, and Individualism is a disturbing and disintegrating force. Therein lies its immense value. For what it seeks to disturb is monotony of type, slavery of custom, tyranny of habit, and the reduction of man to the level of a machine. In Art, the public accept what has been, because they cannot alter it, not because they appreciate it. They swallow their classics whole, and never taste them. They endure them as the inevitable, and as they cannot mar them, they mouth about them. Strangely enough, or not strangely, according to one's own views, this acceptance of the classics does a great deal of harm. The uncritical admiration of the Bible and Shakespeare in England is an instance of what I mean. With regard to the Bible, considerations of ecclesiastical authority enter into the matter, so that I need not dwell upon the point.

But in the case of Shakespeare it is quite obvious that the public really see neither the beauties nor the defects of his plays. If they saw the beauties, they would not object to the development of the drama; and if they saw the defects, they would not object to the development of the drama either. The fact is, the public make use of the classics of a country as a means of checking the progress of Art. They degrade the classics into authorities. They use them as bludgeons for preventing the free expression of Beauty in new forms. They are always asking a writer why he does not write like somebody else, or a painter why he does not paint like somebody else, quite oblivious of the fact that if either of them did anything of the kind he would cease to be an artist. A fresh mode of Beauty is absolutely distasteful to them, and whenever it appears they get so angry and bewildered that they always use two stupid expressions —one is that the work of art is grossly unintelligible; the other, that the work of art is grossly immoral. What they mean by these words seems to me to be this. When they say a work is grossly unintelligible, they mean that the artist has said or made a beautiful thing that is new; when

they describe a work as grossly immoral,
they mean that the artist has said or made
a beautiful thing that is true. The former
expression has reference to style; the latter
to subject-matter. But they probably use
the words very vaguely, as an ordinary
mob will use ready-made paving stones.
There is not a single real poet or prose writer
of this century, for instance, on whom the
British public have not solemnly conferred
diplomas of immorality, and these diplomas
practically take the place, with us, of what
in France is the formal recognition of an
Academy of Letters, and fortunately make
the establishment of such an institution
quite unnecessary in England. Of course,
the public are very reckless in their use of
the word. That they should have called
Wordsworth an immoral poet, was only to
be expected. Wordsworth was a poet.
But that they should have called Charles
Kingsley an immoral novelist is extraordinary. Kingsley's prose was not of a
very fine quality. Still, there is the word,
and they use it as best they can. An artist is, of course, not disturbed by it. The
true artist is a man who believes absolutely
in himself, because he is absolutely himself.
But I can fancy that if an artist produced
a work of art in England that immediately
on its appearance was recognized by the
public, through their medium, which is the
public press, as a work that was quite in-

telligible and highly moral, he would begin to seriously question whether in its creation he had really been himself at all, and consequently whether the work was not quite unworthy of him, and either of a thoroughly second-rate order, or of no artistic value whatsoever.

Perhaps, however, I have wronged the public in limiting them to such words as "immoral," "unintelligible," "exotic," and "unhealthy." There is one other word that they use. That word is "morbid." They do not use it often. The meaning of the word is so simple that they are afraid of using it. Still, they use it sometimes, and, now and then, one comes across it in popular newspapers. It is, of course, a ridiculous word to apply to a work of art. For what is morbidity but a mood of emotion or a mode of thought that one cannot express? The public are all morbid, because the public can never find expression for anything. The artist is never morbid. He expresses everything. He stands outside his subject, and through its medium produces incomparable and artistic effects. To call an artist morbid because he deals with morbidity as his subject-matter is as silly as if one called Shakespeare mad because he wrote "King Lear."

On the whole, an artist in England gains something by being attacked. His individuality is intensified. He becomes more completely himself. Of course, the attacks are very gross, very impertinent, and very contemptible. But then no artist expects grace from the vulgar mind, or style from the suburban intellect. Vulgarity and stupidity are two very vivid facts in modern life. One regrets them, naturally. But there they are. They are subjects for study, like everything else. And it is only fair to state, with regard to modern journalists, that they always apologize to one in private for what they have written against one in public.

Within the last few years two other adjectives, it may be mentioned, have been added to the very limited vocabulary of art-abuse that is at the disposal of the public. One is the word "unhealthy," the other is the word "exotic." The latter merely expresses the rage of the momentary mushroom against the immortal, entrancing, and exquisitely lovely orchid. It is a tribute, but a tribute of no importance. The word "unhealthy," however, admits of analysis. It is a rather interesting word. In fact, it is so interesting that the people who use it do not know what it means.

What does it mean? What is a healthy, or an unhealthy work of art? All terms that one applies to a work of art, provided that one applies them rationally, have reference to either its style or its subject, or to both together. From the point of view of style, a healthy work of art is one whose style recognizes the beauty of the material it employs, be that material one of words or of bronze, of color or of ivory, and uses that beauty as a factor in producing the æsthetic effect. From the point of view of subject, a healthy work of art is one the choice of whose subject is conditioned by the temperament of the artist, and comes directly out of it. In fine, a healthy work of art is one that has both perfection and personality. Of course, form and substance cannot be separted in a work of art; they are always one. But for purposes of analysis, and setting the wholeness of æsthetic impression aside for a moment, we can intellectually so separate them. An unhealthy work of art, on the other hand, is a work whose style is obvious, old-fashioned, and common, and whose subject is deliberately chosen, not because the artist has any pleasure in it, but because he thinks that the public will pay him for it. In fact, the popular novel that the public calls healthy is always a thoroughly unhealthy production; and what the public calls an unhealthy novel is always a beautiful and healthy work of art.

I need hardly say that I am not, for a single moment, complaining that the public and the public press misuse these words. I do not see how, with their lack of comprehension of what Art is, they could pos-

sibly use them in the proper sense. I am
merely pointing out the misuse; and as for
the origin of the misuse and the meaning
that lies behind it all, the explanation is
very simple. It comes from the barbarous
conception of authority. It comes from the
natural inability of a community corrupted
by authority to understand or appreciate
Individualism. In a word, it comes from
that monstrous and ignorant thing that is
called Public Opinion, which, bad and well-
meaning as it is when it tries to control
action, is infamous and of evil meaning
when it tries to control Thought or Art.

Indeed, there is much more to be said
in favor of the physical force of the public
than there is in the favor of the public's
opinion. The former may be fine. The
latter must be foolish. It is often said that
force is no argument. That, however, entirely depends on what one wants to prove.
Many of the most important problems of
the last few centuries, such as the continuance of personal government in England,
or of feudalism in France, have been solved
entirely by means of physical force. The
very violence of a revolution may make the
public grand and splendid for a moment.
It was a fatal day when the public discov-
ered that the pen is mightier than the pav-
ing-stone, and can be made as offensive as
the brickbat. They at once sought for the
journalist, found him, developed him, and

made him their industrious and well-paid servant. It is greatly to be regretted, for both their sakes. Behind the barricade there may be much that is noble and heroic. But what is there behind the leading-article but prejudice, stupidity, cant, and twaddle? And when these four are joined together they make a terrible force, and constitute the new authority.

In old days men had the rack. Now they have the press. That is an improvement certainly. But still it is very bad, and wrong, and demoralizing. Somebody—was it Burke?—called journalism the fourth estate. That was true at the time, no doubt. But at the present moment it really is the only estate. It has eaten up the other three. The Lords Temporal say nothing, the Lords Spiritual have nothing to say, and the House of Commons has nothing to say and says it. We are dominated by Journalism. In America the President reigns for four years, and Journalism governs for ever and ever. Fortunately in America journalism has carried its authority to the grossest and most brutal extreme. As a natural consequence it has begun to create a spirit of revolt. People are amused by it, or disgusted by it, according to their temperaments. But it is no longer the real force it was. It is not seriously treated. In England, Journalism, not, except in a few well-known instances, having been carried to such excesses of brutality, is still a great factor, a really remarkable power. The tyranny that it proposes to exercise over people's private lives seems to me to be quite extraordinary. The fact is, that the public have an insatiable curiosity to know everything, except what is worth knowing. Journalism, conscious of this, and having tradesmen-like habits, supplies their demands. In centuries before ours the public nailed the ears of journalists to the pump. That was quite hideous. In this century journalists have nailed their own ears to the keyhole. That is much worse. And what aggravates the mishief is that the journalists who are most to blame are not the amusing journalists who write for what are called Society papers. The harm is done by the serious, thoughtful, earnest journalists, who solemnly, as they are doing at present, will drag before the eyes of the public some incident in the private life of a great stateman, of a man who is a leader of political thought, and invite the public to discuss the incident, to exercise authority in the matter, to give their views, and not merely to give their views, but to carry them into action, to dictate to the man upon all other points, to dictate to his party, to dictate to his country; in fact, to make themselves ridiculous, offensive, and harmful. The private lives of men and women should not be told to the public. The pub-

lic have nothing to do with them at all.
In France they manage these things better.
There they do not allow the details of the
trials that take place in the divorce courts
to be published for the amusement or criticism of the public. All that the public are
allowed to know is that the divorce has
taken place and was granted on petition of
one or other or both of the married parties
concerned. In France, in fact, they limit
the journalist, and allow the artist almost
perfect freedom. Here we allow absolute
freedom to the journalist, and entirely limit
the artist. English public opinion, that is
to say, tries to constrain and impede and
warp the man who makes things that are
beautiful in effect, and compels the journalist to retail things that are ugly, or disgusting, or revolting in fact, so that we have
the most serious journalists in the world,
and the most indecent newspapers. It is
no exaggeration to talk of compulsion.
There are possibly some journalists who
take a real pleasure in publishing horrible
things, or who, being poor, look to scandals
as forming a sort of permanent basis for
an income. But there are other journalists,
I feel certain, men of education and cultiva-
tion, who really dislike publishing these
things, who know that it is wrong to do
so, and only do it because the unhealthy
conditions under which their occupation is
carried on oblige them to supply the pub-

lic with what the public wants, and to compete with other journalists in making that supply as full and satisfying to the gross popular appetite as possible. It is a very degrading position for any body of educated men to be placed in, and I have no doubt that most of them feel it acutely.

However, let us leave what is really a very sordid side of the subject, and return to the question of popular control in the matter of Art, by which I mean Public Opinion dictating to the artist the form which he is to use, the mode in which he is to use it, and the materials with which he is to work. I have pointed out that the arts which have escaped best in England are the arts in which the public have not been interested. They are, however, interested in the drama, and as a certain advance has been made in the drama within the last ten or fifteen years, it is important to point out that this advance is entirely due to a few individual artists refusing to accept the popular want of taste as their standard, and refusing to regard Art as a mere matter of demand and supply. With his marvelous and vivid personality, with a style that has really a true color-element in it, with his extraordinary power, not over mere mimicry, but over imaginative and intellectual creation, Mr. Irving, had his sole object been to give the public what they wanted, could have produced the com-

monest plays in the commonest manner, and
made as much success and money as a man
could possibly desire. But his object was
not that. His object was to realize his own
perfection as an artist, under certain conditions, and in certain forms of Art. At
first he appealed to the few: now he has
educated the many. He has created in the
public both taste and temperament. The
public appreciate his artistic success im-
mensely. I often wonder, however, whether the public understand that that success
is entirely due to the fact that he did not
accept their standard, but realized his own.
With their standard the Lyceum would
have been a sort of second-rate booth, as
some of the popular theatres in London are
at present. Whether they understand it or
not the fact however remains, that taste
and temperament have, to a certain extent,
been created in the public, and that the
public is capable of developing these quali-
ties. The problem then is, why do not the
public become more civilized? They have
the capacity. What stops them?

The thing that stops them, it must be
said again, is their desire to exercise authority over the artist and over works of
art. To certain theatres, such as the
Lyceum and the Haymarket, the public
seem to come in a proper mood. In both
of these theatres there have been individual
artists, who have succeeded in creating in

their audiences—and every theatre in London has its own audience—the temperament to which Art appeals. And what is that temperament? It is the temperament of receptivity. That is all.

If a man approaches a work of art with any desire to exercise authority over it and the artist, he approaches it in such a spirit that he cannot receive any artistic impression from it at all. The work of art is to dominate the spectator: the spectator is not to dominate the work of art. The spectator is to be receptive. He is to be the violin on which the master is to play. And the more completely he can suppress his own silly views, his own foolish prejudices, his own absurd ideas of what Art should be, or should not be, the more likely he is to understand and appreciate the work of art in question. This is, of course, quite obvious in the case of the vulgar theatre-going public of English men and women. But it is equally true of what are called educated people. For an educated person's ideas of Art are drawn naturally from what Art has been, whereas the new work of Art is beautiful by being what Art has never been; and to measure it by the standard of the past is to measure it by a standard on the rejection of which its real perfection depends. A temperament capable of receiving, through an imaginative medium, and under imaginative conditions, new and beautiful impressions, is the only temperament that can appreciate a work of art. And true as this is in the case of the appreciation of sculpture and painting, it is still more true of the appreciation of such arts as the drama. For a picture and a statue are not at war with Time. They take no count of its succession. In one moment their unity may be apprehended. In the case of literature it is different. Time must be traversed before the unity of effect is realized. And so, in the drama, there may occur in the first act of the play something whose real artistic value may not be evident to the spectator till the third or fourth act is reached. Is the silly fellow to get angry and call out, and disturb the play, and annoy the artists? No. The honest man is to sit quietly, and know the delightful emotions of wonder, curiosity, and suspense. He is not to go to the play to lose a vulgar temper. He is to go to the play to realize an artistic temperament. He is to go to the play to gain an artistic temperament. He is not the arbiter of the work of art. He is one who is admitted to contemplate the work of art, and, if the work be fine, to forget in its contemplation all the egotism that mars him—the egotism of his ignorance, or the egotism of his information. This point about the drama is hardly, I think, sufficiently recognized. I can quite understand that were "Macbeth"

produced for the first time before a modern
London audience, many of the people present would strongly and vigorously object
to the introduction of the witches in the
first act, with their grotesque phrases and
their ridiculous words. But when the play
is over one realizes that the laughter of the
witches in "Macbeth" is as terrible as the
laughter of madness in "Lear," more terrible than the laughter of Iago in the tragedy
of the Moor. No spectator of art needs a
more perfect mood of receptivity than the
spectator of a play. The moment he seeks
to exercise authority he becomes the
avowed enemy of Art and of himself. Art
does not mind. It is he who suffers.

With the novel it is the same thing.
Popular authority and the recognition of
popular authority are fatal. Thackeray's
"Esmond" is a beautiful work of art because he wrote it to please himself. In his
other novels, in "Pendennis," in "Philip,"
in "Vanity Fair" even, at times, he is too
conscious of the public, and spoils his work
by appealing directly to the sympathies of
the public, or by directly mocking at them.
A true artist takes no notice whatever of
the public. The public are to him non-
existent. He has no poppied or honeyed
cakes through which to give the monster
sleep or sustenance. He leaves that to the
popular novelist. One incomparable novelist we have now in England, Mr. George

Meredith. There are better artists in France, but France has no one whose view of life is so large, so varied, so imaginatively true. There are tellers of stories in Russia who have a more vivid sense of what pain in fiction may be. But to him belongs philosophy in fiction. His people not merely live, but they live in thought. One can see them from myriad points of view. They are suggestive. There is soul in them and around them. They are interpretative and symbolic. And he who made them, those wonderful quickly-moving figures, made them for his own pleasure, and has never asked the public what they wanted, has never cared to know what they wanted, has never allowed the public to dictate to him or influence him in any way, but has gone on intensifying his own personality, and producing his own individual work. At first none came to him. That did not matter. Then the few came to him. That did not change him. The many have come now. He is still the same. He is an incomparable novelist.

With the decorative arts it is not different. The public clung with really pathetic tenacity to what I believe were the direct traditions of the Great Exhibition of international vulgarity, traditions that were so appalling that the houses in which people lived were only fit for blind people to live in. Beautiful things began to be made, beautiful colors came from the dyer's hand, beautiful patterns from the artist's brain, and the use of beautiful things and their value and importance were set forth. The public were really very indignant. They lost their temper. They said silly things. No one minded. No one was a whit the worse. No one accepted the authority of public opinion. And now it is almost impossible to enter any modern house without seeing some recognition of good taste, some recognition of the value of lovely surroundings, some sign of appreciation of beauty. In fact, people's houses are, as a rule, quite charming nowadays. People have been to a very great extent civilized. It is only fair to state, however, that the extraordinary success of the revolution in house-decoration and furniture and the like has not really been due to the majority of the public developing a very fine taste in such matters. It has been chiefly due to the fact that the craftsmen of things so appreciated the pleasure of making what was beautiful, and woke to such a vivid consciousness of the hideousness and vulgarity of what the public had previously wanted, that they simply starved the public out. It would be quite impossible at the present moment to furnish a room as rooms were furnished a few years ago, without going for everything to an auction of second-hand furniture from some third-rate lodging-house. The things are no longer made. However they may object to it, people must nowadays have something charming in their surroundings. Fortunately for them, their assumption of authority in these art-matters came to entire grief.

It is evident, then, that all authority in such things is bad. People sometimes inquire what form of government is most suitable for an artist to live under. To this question there is only one answer. The form of government that is most suitable to the artist is no government at all. Authority over him and his art is ridiculous. It has been stated that under despotisms artists have produced lovely work. This is not quite so. Artists have visited despots, not as subjects to be tyrannized over, but as wandering wonder-makers, as fascinating vagrant personalities, to be entertained and charmed and suffered to be at peace, and allowed to create. There is this to be said in favor of the despot, that he, being an individual, may have culture, while the mob, being a monster, has none. One who is an Emperor and King may stoop down to pick up a brush for a painter, but when the democracy stoops down it is merely to throw mud. And yet the democracy have not so far to stoop as the emperor. In fact, when they want to throw mud they have not to stoop at all. But there is no necessity to separate the monarch from the mob; all authority is equally bad.

There are three kinds of despots. There is the despot who tyrannizes over the body. There is the despot who tyrannizes over the soul. There is the despot who tyrannizes over the soul and body alike. The first is called the Prince. The second is called the Pope. The third is called the People. The Prince may be cultivated. Many Princes have been. Yet in the Prince there is danger. One thinks of Dante at the bitter feast in Verona, of Tasso in Ferrara's madman's cell. It is better for the artist not to live with Princes. The Pope may be cultivated. Many Popes have been; the bad Popes have been. The bad Popes loved Beauty, almost as passionately, nay, with as much passion as the good Popes hated Thought. To the wickedness of the Papacy humanity owes much. The goodness of the Papacy owes a terrible debt to humanity. Yet, though the Vatican has kept the rhetoric of its thunders, and lost the rod of its lightning, it is better for the artist not to live with Popes. It was a Pope who said of Cellini to a conclave of Cardinals that common laws and common authority were not made for men such as he; but it was a Pope who thrust Cellini into prison, and kept him there till he sickened with rage, and created unreal visions for himself, and saw the gilded sun enter his room, and

grew so enamoured of it that he sought to
escape, and crept out from tower to tower,
and falling through dizzy air at dawn,
maimed himself, and was by a vine-dresser
covered with vine leaves, and carried in
a cart to one who, loving beautiful things,
had cared of him. There is danger in
Popes.

And as for the People, what of them
and their authority? Perhaps of them and
their authority one has spoken enough.
Their authority is a thing blind, deaf,
hideous, grotesque, tragic, amusing, serious,
and obscene. It is impossible for the artist
to live with the People. All despots bribe.
The people bribe and brutalize. Who told
them to exercise authority? They were
made to live, to listen, and to love. Some-
one has done them a great wrong. They
have marred themselves by imitation of
their inferiors. They have taken the
sceptre of the Prince. How should they
use it? They have taken the triple tiara of
the Pope. How should they carry its burden? They are as a clown whose heart is
broken. They are as a priest whose soul
is not yet born. Let all who love Beauty
pity them. Though they themselves love
not Beauty, yet let them pity themselves.
Who taught them the trick of tyranny?

There are many other things that one
might point out. One might point out
how the Renaissance was great, because it

sought to solve no social problem, and busied itself not about such things, but suffered the individual to develop freely, beautifully, and naturally, and so had great and individual artists, and great and individual men. One might point out how Louis XIV., by creating the modern state, destroyed the individualism of the artist, and made things monstrous in their monotony of repetition, and contemptible in their conformity to rule, and destroyed throughout all France all those fine freedoms of expression that had made tradition new in beauty, and new modes one with antique form. But the past is of no importance. The present is of no importance. It is with the future that we have to deal. For the past is what man should not have been. The present is what man ought not to be. The future is what artists are.

It will, of course, be said that such a scheme as is set forth here is quite unpractical, and goes against human nature. This is perfectly true. It is unpractical, and it goes against human nature. This is why it is worth carrying out, and that is why one proposes it. For what is a practical scheme? A practical scheme is either a scheme that is already in existence, or a scheme that could be carried out under existing conditions But it is exactly the existing conditions that one objects to; and any scheme that could accept these condi-

tions is wrong and foolish. The conditions
will be done away with, and human nature
will change. The only thing that one really
knows about human nature is that it
changes. Change is the one quality we
can predicate of it. The systems that fail
are those that rely on the permanency of
human nature, and not on its growth and
development. The error of Louis XIV.
was that he thought human nature would
always be the same. The result of his error
was the French Revolution. It was an admirable result. All the results of the mis-
takes of governments are quite admirable.

It is to be noted also that Individualism
does not come to man with any sickly
cant about duty, which merely means doing what other people want because they
want it; or any hideous cant about self-
sacrifice, which is merely a survival of sav-
age mutilation. In fact, it does not come
to man with any claims upon him at all.
It comes naturally and inevitably out of
man. It is the point to which all development tends. It is the differentiation to
which all organisms grow. It is the perfection that is inherent in every mode of
life, and towards which every mode of life
quickens. And so Individualism exercises
no compulsion over man. On the contrary,
it says to man that he should suffer no compulsion to be exercised over him. It does
not try to force people to be good. It

knows that people are good when they are
let alone. Man will develop Individualism
out of himself. Man is now so developing
Individualism. To ask whether Individualism is practical is like asking whether Evolution is practical. Evolution is the law of
life, and there is no evolution except towards Individualism. Where this tendency
is not expressed, it is a case of artificially-
arrested growth, or of disease, or of death.

Individualism will also be unselfish and
unaffected. It has been pointed out that
one of the results of the extraordinary
tyranny of authority is that words are absolutely distorted from their proper and
simple meaning, and are used to express
the obverse of their right signification.
What is true about Art is true about Life.
A man is called affected, nowadays, if he
dresses as he likes to dress. But in doing
that he is acting in a perfectly natural manner. Affectation, in such matters, consists
in dressing according to the views of one's
neighbor, whose views, as they are the
views of the majority, will probably be
extremely stupid. Or a man is called
selfish if he lives in the manner that seems
to him most suitable for the full realization
of his own personality; if, in fact, the
primary aim of life is self-development. But
this is the way in which everyone should
live. Selfishness is not living as one wishes
to live, it is asking others to live as one

wishes to live. And unselfishness is letting other people's lives alone, not interfering with them. Selfishness always aims at creating around it an absolute uniformity of type. Unselfishness recognizes infinite variety of type as a delightful thing, accepts it, acquiesces in it, enjoys it. It is not selfish to think for oneself. A man who does not think for himself does not think at all. It is grossly selfish to require of one's neighbor that he should think in the same way, and hold the same opinions. Why should he ? If he can think, he will probably think differently. If he cannot think, it is monstrous to require thought of any kind from him. A red rose is not selfish because it wants to be a red rose. It would be horribly selfish if it wanted all the other flowers in the garden to be both red and roses. Under Individualism people will be quite natural and absolutely unselfish, and will know the meanings of the words, and realize them in their free, beautiful lives. Nor will men be egotistic as they are now. For the egotist is he who makes claims upon others, and the Individualist will not desire to do that. It will not give him pleasure. When man has realized Individualism, he will also realize sympathy and exercise it freely and spontaneously. Up to the present man has hardly cultivated sympathy at all. He has merely sympathy with pain, and sympathy

with pain is not the highest form of sympathy. All sympathy is fine, but sympathy
with suffering is the least fine mode. It is
tainted with egotism. It is apt to become
morbid. There is in it a certain element of
terror for our own safety. We become
afraid that we ourselvse might be as the
leper or as the blind, and that no man
would have care of us. It is curiously
limiting, too. One should sympathize with
the entirety of life, not with life's sores
and maladies merely, but with life's joy
and beauty and energy and health and freedom. The wider sympathy is, of course, the
more difficult. It requires more unselfishness. Anybody can sympathize with the
sufferings of a friend, but it requires a
very fine nature—it requires, in fact, the
nature of a true Individualist—to sympathize with a friend's success. In the modern
stress of competition and struggle for place,
such sympathy is naturally rare, and is also
very much stifled by the immoral idea of
uniformity of type and conformity to rule
which is so prevalent everywhere, and is
perhaps most obnoxious in England.

Sympathy with pain there will, of course,
always be. It is one of the first instincts
of man. The animals which are individual,
the higher animals, that is to say, share it
with us. But it must be remembered that
while sympathy with joy intensifies the sum
of joy in the world, sympathy with pain

does not really diminish the amount of pain.
It may make man better able to endure evil,
but the evil remains. Sympathy with consumption does not cure consumption; that
is what Science does. And when Socialism
has solved the problem of poverty, and Science solved the problem of disease, the area
of the sentimentalists will be lessened, and
the sympathy of man will be large, healthy,
and spontaeous. Man will have joy in
the contemplation of the joyous lives of
others.

For it is through joy that the Individualism of the future will develop itself.
Christ made no attempt to reconstruct society, and consequently the Individualism
that he preached to man could be realized
only through pain or in solitude. The ideals
that we owe to Christ are the ideals of the
man who abandons society entirely, or of
the man who resists society absolutely. But
man is naturally social. Even the The-
baid became peopled at last. And though
the cenobite realizes his personality, it is
often an impoverished personality that he
realizes. Upon the other hand, the terrible
truth that pain is a mode through which
man may realize himself exercises a wonderful fascination over the world. Shallow
speakers and shallow thinkers in pulpits
and on platforms often talk about the
world's worship of pleasure, and whine
against it. But it is rarely in the world's

history that its ideal has been one of joy
and beauty. The worship of pain has far
more often dominated the world. Mediævalism, with its saints and martyrs, its love
of self-torture, its wild passion for wound-
ing itself, its gashing with knives, and its
whipping with rods—Mediævalism is real
Christianity, and the mediæval Christ is the
real Christ. When the Renaissance dawn-
ed upon the world, and brought with it the
new ideals of the beauty of life and the joy
of living, men could not understand Christ.
Even Art shows us that. The painters of
the Renaissance drew Christ as a little boy
playing with another boy in a palace or a
garden, or lying back in his mother's arms,
smiling at her, or at a flower, or at a bright
bird; or as a noble, stately figure moving
nobly through the world; or as a wonderful
figure rising in a sort of ecstasy from death
to life. Even when they drew him cruci-
fied they drew him as a beautiful God on
whom evil men had inflicted suffering. But
he did not preoccupy them much. What
delighted them was to paint the men and
women whom they admired, and to show
the loveliness of this lovely earth. They
painted many religious pictures—in fact,
they painted far too many, and the monotony of type and motive is wearisome, and
was bad for art. It was the result of the
authority of the public in art-matters, and
is to be deplored. But their soul was not

in the subject. Raphael was a great artist
when he painted his portrait of the Pope.
When he painted his Madonnas and infant
Christs, he is not a great artist at all.
Christ had no message for the Renaissance,
which was wonderful because it brought an
ideal at variance with his, and to find the
presentation of the real Christ we must go
to mediæval art. There he is one maimed
and marred; one who is not comely to look
on, because Beauty is a joy; one who is not
in fair raiment, because that may be a joy
also: he is a beggar who has a marvelous
soul; he ls a leper whose soul is divine; he
needs neither property nor health; he is a
God realizing his perfection through pain.

The evolution of man is slow. The injustice of men is great. It was necessary
that pain should be put forward as a mode
of self-realization. Even now, in some
places in the world, the message of Christ
is necessary. No one who lived in modern
Russia could possibly realize his perfection
except by pain. A few Russian artists have
realized themselves in Art, in a fiction that
is mediæval in character, because its domi-
nant note is the realization of men through
suffering. But for those who are not artists, and to whom there is no mode of life
but the actual life of fact, pain is the only
door to perfection. A Russian who lives
happily under the present system of government in Russia must either believe that

man has no soul, or that, if he has, it is not worth developing. A Nihilist who rejects all authority, because he knows authority to be evil, and who welcomes all pain, because through that he realizes his personality, is a real Christian. To him the Christian ideal is a true thing.

And yet, Christ did not revolt against authority. He accepted the imperial authority of the Roman Empire and paid tribute. He endured the ecclesiastical authority of the Jewish Church, and would not repel its violence by any violence of his own. He had, as I said before, no scheme for the reconstruction of society. But the modern world has schemes. It proposes to do away with poverty and the suffering that it entails. It desires to get rid of pain, and the suffering that pain entails. It trusts to Socialism and to Science as its methods. What it aims at is an Individualism expressing itself through joy. This Individualism will be larger, fuller, lovelier than any Individualism has ever been. Pain is not the ultimate mode of perfection. It is merely provisional and a protest. It has reference to wrong, unhealthy, unjust surroundings. When the wrong, and the disease, and the injustice are removed, it will have no further place. It will have done its work. It was a great work, but it is almost over. Its sphere lessens every day.

Nor will man miss it. For what man

has sought for is, indeed, neither pain nor pleasure, but simply Life. Man has sought to live intensely, fully, perfectly. When he can do so without exercising restraint on others, or suffering it ever, and his activities are all pleasurable to him, he will be saner, healthier, more civilized, more himself. Pleasure is Nature's test, her sign of approval. When man is happy, he is in harmony with himself and his environment. The new Individualism, for whose service Socialism, whether it wills it or not, is working, will be perfect harmony. It will be what the Greeks sought for, but could not except in Thought realize completely, because they had slaves, and fed them; it will be what the Renaissance sought for, but could not realize completely except in Art, because they had slaves, and starved them. It will be complete, and through it each man will attain to his perfection. The new Individualism is the new Hellenism.

PUBLISHER'S NOTE

The Soul of Man Under Socialism
by Oscar Wilde
was first published in England in 1895.

★

This edition is a facsimile reprint
of the edition published by Max Maisel
in New York, 1911.

★

The photograph of Wilde
reproduced on the cover
was taken by Sarony
in 1882.

★

The sketch of Wilde by Arthur Cravan
reproduced here as a frontispiece
originally appeared in the third issue
of Cravan's review *Maintenant,*
(Paris, October-November, 1913).

★

ISBN 0-88286-056-9
Also available in a cloth edition
cloth ISBN 0-88286-056-7

The Flivver King: A story of Ford-America
by Upton Sinclair
A classic novel portraying the rise of Henry Ford's automotive empire and the origins of the United Auto Workers. First published in 1937, it remains one of the best studies of Ford and Fordism. With a new introduction by Steve Meyer. $7.95

You Have No Country! Workers' Struggle Against War
by Mary E. Marcy
A collection of anti-war articles by the editor of the *International Socialist Review* during World War I. Eugene Debs called Marcy "one of the clearest minds and greatest souls in all our movement." Her critique of imperialist war and her strategy for ending war are still as timely as ever. With an introduction by Franklin Rosemont. $4.95

Mister Block
by Ernest Riebe
A facsimile reprint of the first radical comic book, a hilarious collection published by the Industrial Workers of the World in 1913. The original today is practically impossible to find, even in libraries. Inspired by this comic, Joe Hill wrote one of his most popular songs. $4.95

A Sketch of the Life of Thomas Skidmore
by Amos Gilbert
A short biography, originally published in 1834, of the man who organized the first American revolutionary workers' group, the "Agrarian" faction of the New York City Workingmen's Party, in 1829. With an introduction by Mark Lause. $3.95

Proudhon and His Bank of the People
by Charles A. Dana
Originally published in 1849, this is the first American study devoted to the "Father of Anarchism." This facsimile of Benjamin Tucker's 1896 edition includes Tucker's preface, and a new introduction by Paul Avrich. $4.95

Charles H. Kerr Publishing Company
Established 1886
1740 Greenleaf Avenue, Suite 7
Chicago, Illinois 60626